Nuns So Lovable

cartoons by
Joe Lane

published by About Comics, Camarillo, California

Nuns So Lovelable
Originally published by Michael Book Co., 1957
About Comics edition published April, 2018

Customized editions available

Send all queries to *questions@aboutcomics.com*

"Please, St. Jude, do the impossible!"

"Offhand, Sister Dorothea, I'd say you're making marvelous progress here!"

"Promoted to third grade - - - my, my,
you've come a long way, Turibius!"

"Sister Adora, is this one of the many ills the flesh is heir to?"

"Please, Cub Scouts, not in uniform!"

"Now watch — they'll ask for some island no one has ever heard of!"

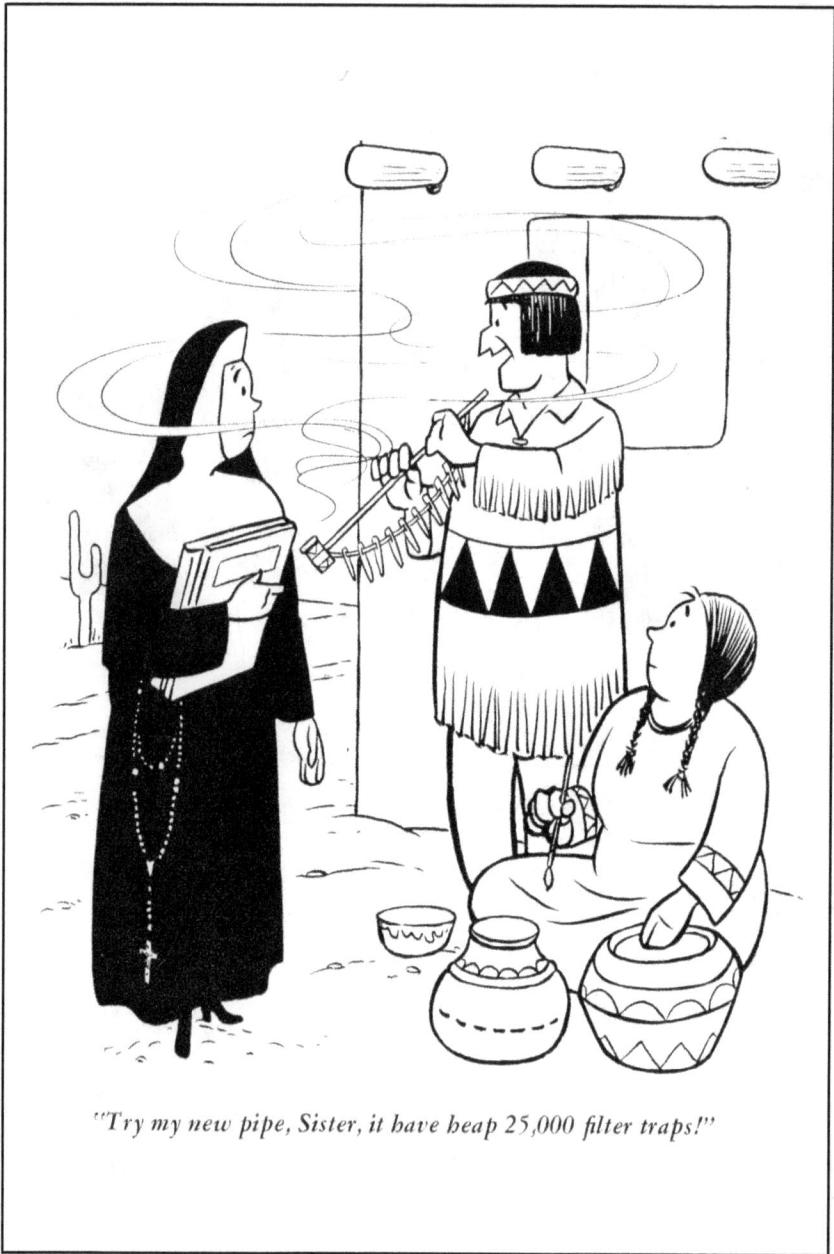

"Try my new pipe, Sister, it have heap 25,000 filter traps!"

"And this is the big sizzler from the gridiron!"

"This, I assume, is the automatic dryer."

"And what did you do in civilian life, Kenny?"

"And here, Sister Adrian, is our walk-up apartment."

"Yes, I have a question — may we have that box when you're finished?"

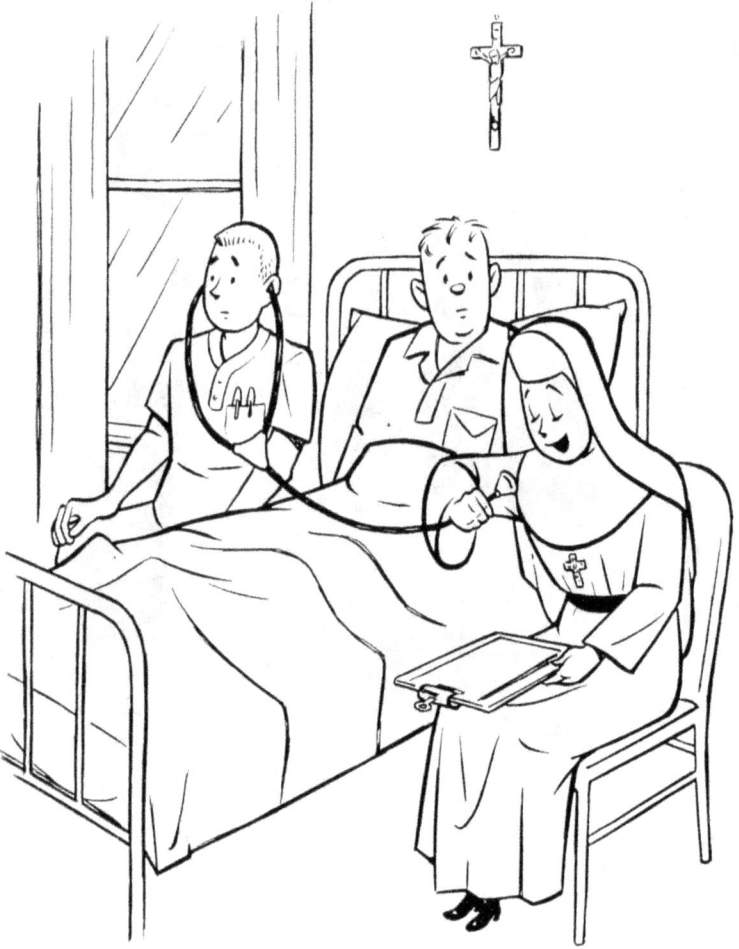

"Roger, over and out!"

"Pass out these papers, Milton, and let neither snow nor rain nor heat nor gloom of night stay you from the swift completion of your appointed rounds."

"Do we pay for it in this world or can we wait 'til the next?"

"Sister Ignatia, is that the Doctor driving in the needle?"

"Methodius always said he'd have his own business some day."

"Sister says I do things to a piano that no one else can do!"

"There are twenty-three of us and we must have our potatoes
all the same size."

"I keep getting the busy signal, Sister."

"Sister Willene is very impartial. No one gets a hundred!"

"The time? Oh, I guess it's about July or August, Sister."

"You be my beneficiary, Sister, and I'll be yours!"

"We just want you to know we're happy with all our presents!"

"And this is our wash machine, Sister."

"I don't know, Dominic. It just doesn't sound right!"

"Could we watch the Notre Dame game while we make up our mind?"

"I don't know, Sister, but I thought the book was much better!"

"I know, Sister Sulpice, I'm late — l-a-t."

"Remember now, the truth, the whole truth and nothing but, so help you!"

"Do you have 'Three O'Clock in the Morning' and 'Feather Your Nest?' "

"Before we go to Midnight Services, Reverend Mother, would it be permissible to give one toot?"

"But, Sister Dorothea, everyone wears make-up on TV!"

"Believe me, if I had my life to live over again, I'd be a nun!"

"We were sort of toying with the idea of Black!"

"Expect to stay long?"

"Please, Miss, where can we find the exit?"

"Sister, are you from Mars?"

"Don't forget, Sister, drop in any time."

"Now there, no doubt, Sister Grace, is something fraught with meaning!"

"Give us everything that's free!"

"Oh, we stick pretty close to home!"

"Who—er—whom shall I say is calling, Sister?"

"Oh, Sister, you shouldn't have — I have everything!"

"Er, could we have a peanut butter and jelly on rye?"

"After taking your medicine, Doctor, and making a novena to St. Peregrine, I feel wonderful!"

"Almost broke my perfect attendance record today, Sister!"

"Oh, well — thy will be done!"

'Do you really think she's got eyes in the back of her head?'

"Listen, Sister, he's playing our song!"

"Sister Fridian, I think the pilot light is out in this stove!"

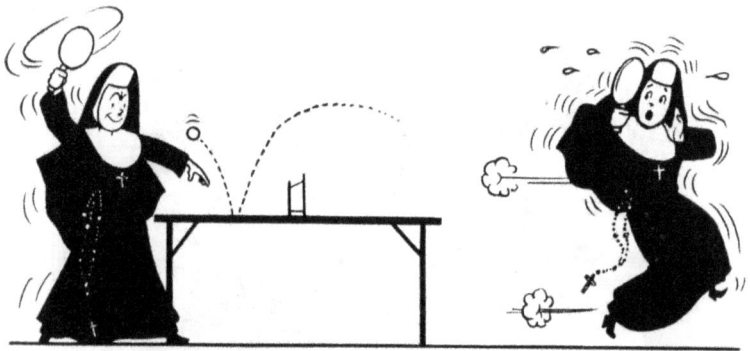

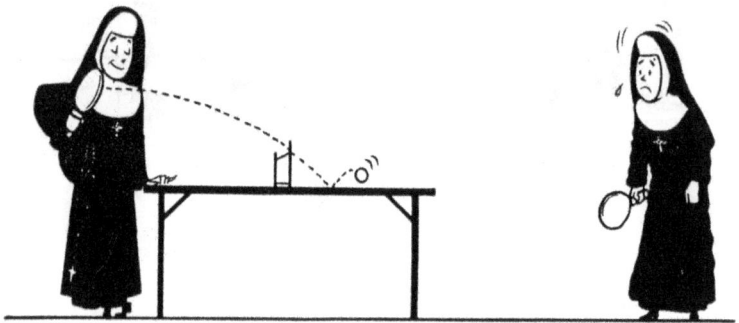

"You take this house, Sister Ervin. I'll go next door."

"Peter and Thomas, stop that talking!"

"And unless you come up with a win today, I'll be back teaching kindergarten!"

"Sister Thomas More, may we choose our category?"

"Your logic is profoundly conclusive, Camillus—"

"And you justify your point of view very convincingly—"

"But you still must do homework!"

"Under the spreading chestnut tree,
the village smithy stands, engaged
in a rather out-moded form of employment."

"It says I'll be a great success and have lots of children!"

Get all our little books of Joe Lane's little nuns

Our Little Nuns
More Little Nuns
Nuns So Lovable
Vale of Dears
Yes, Sister! No, Sister!

or get

The Big Book of Nun Cartoons
a lifetime supply all in one volume!

Look for them where you got this book,
or visit www.AboutComics.com

Classic Cartoon Collections!

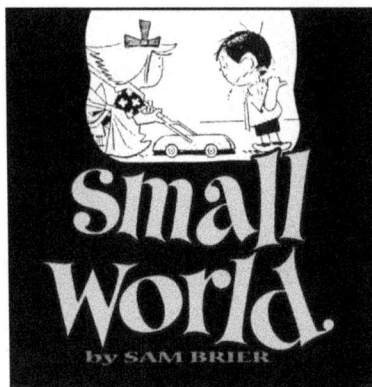

Small World
by SAM BRIER

Sam Brier's 1950s quirky comic strip is about kids playing as adults... or adults drawn as kids.

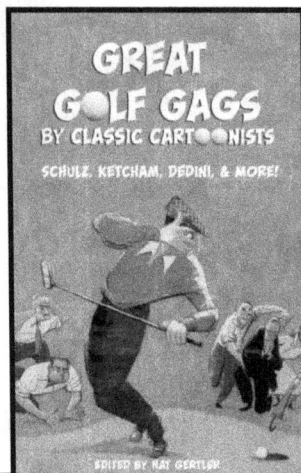

GREAT GOLF GAGS
BY CLASSIC CARTOONISTS
SCHULZ, KETCHAM, DEDINI, & MORE!

EDITED BY RAY GERTLER

Golf cartoons by Hank Ketcham, Eldon Dedini, Virgil Partch, Bill O'Malley, & more

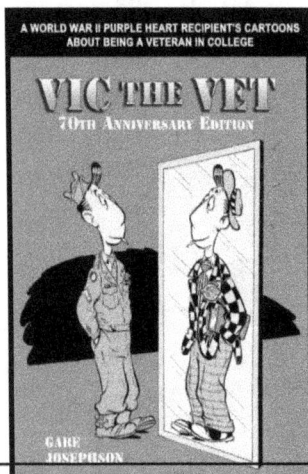

A WORLD WAR II PURPLE HEART RECIPIENT'S CARTOONS ABOUT BEING A VETERAN IN COLLEGE

VIC THE VET
70TH ANNIVERSARY EDITION

GARE JOSEPHSON

Cartoons about being a World War II vet at college on the GI Bill... by a World War II vet while at college.

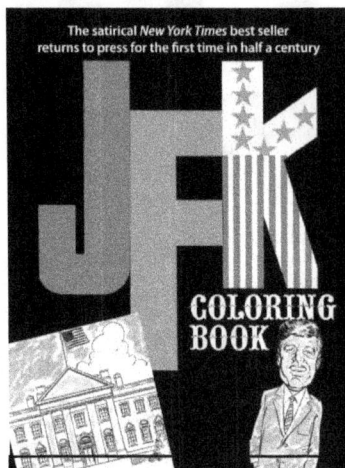

The satirical *New York Times* best seller returns to press for the first time in half a century

JFK COLORING BOOK

Mort Drucker illustrates this New York Times best-seller